POLYCARP
OF SMYRNA

The Man Whose Faith Lasted

Heroes of the Faith

THE BANNER OF TRUTH TRUST
3 Murrayfield Road, Edinburgh EH12 6EL, UK
P.O. Box 621, Carlisle, PA 17013, USA

*

© Sinclair B. Ferguson 2010

*

ISBN-13: 978 1 84871 092 4

*

Typeset in Times New Roman 15/18 at
The Banner of Truth Trust, Edinburgh

Printed in the U.S.A. by
Versa Press, Inc.,
East Peoria, IL

*

Scripture quotations are from The Holy Bible, English Standard Version,
copyright © 2001 by Crossway Bibles, a publishing ministry of Good News Publishers.
Used by permission. All rights reserved.

POLYCARP

OF SMYRNA

THE MAN WHOSE FAITH LASTED

SINCLAIR B. FERGUSON

ILLUSTRATED BY ALISON BROWN

THE BANNER OF TRUTH TRUST

TABLE OF CONTENTS

IN THE ARENA	P. 7
POLYCARP'S MEMORIES	P. 8
MEMORY 1. CHILDHOOD	P. 8
MEMORY 2. JOHN	P. 12
MEMORY 3. TWO FRIENDS	P. 15
INTO THE ARENA	P. 19
FAITHFUL TO JESUS	P. 24
LEARNING FROM POLYCARP	P. 33
ABOUT POLYCARP OF SMYRNA	P. 35
TIMELINE	P. 36
A PERSONAL WORD TO PARENTS	P. 39

IN THE ARENA

THE old man walked slowly into the centre of the arena. The stadium in the city of Smyrna was full of people. This was the man the crowd had been waiting to see. There he was, standing in front of them for the first time . . . This was the famous Polycarp.

POLYCARP had never seen so many people in one place. He couldn't count them all. There must have been 20,000, or even more.
Suddenly the crowd started chanting. The noise grew louder and louder until it filled the air and was all around him. They were chanting his name . . .
'Po-ly-carp! Po-ly-carp!'

HE knew it would not be long now. The shouts of the crowd were deafening. But somehow it did not seem to trouble Polycarp. His mind was elsewhere. He was thinking to himself: 'Why do my memories of things that have happened to me always come in groups of three?'

Polycarp's Memories

Memory 1. Childhood

For a moment Polycarp thought back to the time when he was just a young boy. There he was with his mother and father who loved him very much.

Polycarp had always known that his family was different from other people.

People watched them when they were walking in the city streets.

They often called his parents a name.

'Look', they said to one another, that man and his wife are Christians.'

When people said that, Polycarp always gripped his father's hand tighter. He knew that the Roman Emperors did not like Christians.

POLYCARP lived in Smyrna. It was a large city in the Roman province of Asia.

Each Sunday his parents took him to a place where they met with other Christians and their children. There they used to read from the Bible and sing hymns to the Lord Jesus.

POLYCARP couldn't remember the first time he heard about the Saviour. He felt as if he had always known him.

Polycarp's mother and father had taught him about God.

He remembered how they used to tell him about Jesus every day!

He loved to hear what Jesus had taught. He wanted to trust the Lord Jesus and do what he said.

JESUS had lived when Polycarp's grandfather had been a young man.
Jesus had been killed by the Romans outside Jerusalem, but three days later he had risen from the dead.

ONE of Jesus' disciples had come to Smyrna. His name was John and he had taught Polycarp's father and mother about Jesus. He told them that Jesus had died in their place to take away their sins. Jesus had risen from the dead to give them new life.

IT was a long time ago that Polycarp had first trusted in Jesus.

When he grew up he became a minister of the church in Smyrna.

It was sometimes dangerous to be a follower of Jesus in the city of Smyrna.

MEMORY 2. JOHN

POLYCARP was still standing in the arena. Now a second memory came flooding back! The Apostle John! How could Polycarp ever forget his first meeting with John?

JOHN had been with Jesus and had written an amazing book called a Gospel. Even before he met him, Polycarp had heard stories about Jesus from John's Gospel. But then Polycarp met John himself!

JOHN had described how Jesus had done many amazing things. He had healed the sick. He had made the blind see.

John used to say with a smile, 'All the libraries in the world could not hold the books I could write about Jesus!'

BUT best of all, Jesus had died for Polycarp's sins.

How marvellous to be taught by someone who had been with Jesus!

JOHN had also taught Polycarp that the most important thing was to trust in Jesus for himself.

> Other people had also known John and had heard him speak about Jesus — but they didn't trust in the Lord for themselves.
>
> John wanted to be sure that Polycarp trusted in Jesus for himself . . . and he did!

THE APOSTLE JOHN

SOME time after this, John was arrested for being a disciple of Jesus and was sent away to a remote island called Patmos.

While he was there, God gave him a wonderful vision. In that vision the Lord Jesus told him to write seven different letters. They were to be sent to seven churches. One of these letters was sent to the church in Smyrna.*

These are the words of Jesus, the First and the Last, who died and came to life.

I know your troubles. I know you are poor (but really you are rich!). I know that some people speak against you . . . They really belong to Satan. Do not be afraid of what you are going to suffer. Listen carefully. The Devil is about to throw some of you in prison. This is a test. For a number of days there will be difficulties.

Remember this: Be faithful unto death. If you are, I will give you the crown of life. Listen carefully to what I am telling you. The one who conquers will not be hurt by the second death.

AS Polycarp remembered these things he said to himself, 'God has been very good to me. I have met some amazing disciples of Jesus.'

---

* See Revelation chapter 2 verses 8-11.

MEMORY 3. TWO FRIENDS

IN the stadium Polycarp's friends wondered if all the noise had made him deaf since he did not seem to hear the crowd.

In fact his mind was on other things. He was thinking about two old friends.

For a moment he thought about his young friend Irenaeus. He had taught him years ago. What was he doing now?

Then the other face flashed into his mind. Ignatius! How long it seemed since he had last seen Ignatius. Polycarp wasn't sure how long it was; but it didn't really matter now.

NEXT to John, Ignatius was the most amazing man Polycarp had ever known. He had never met anyone quite like him.

Ignatius actually seemed to want to die for Jesus.

The Christians called a person who died for Jesus a 'martyr'. 'Martyr' comes from the Greek word meaning 'witness'.

POLYCARP remembered that Ignatius had told him to be brave for Jesus.

What would Ignatius say if he could talk to Polycarp today?

POLYCARP had kept a letter Ignatius had once sent him.

He had read it again only a couple of hours ago.

Polycarp had made copies of this precious letter, but he had taken the original letter with him.

HE stopped for a moment, reached inside his robe and took the letter out to read once more.

Polycarp had read it so often that he knew it by heart.

But he wanted to read his favourite words again.

Yes, there they were, in the handwriting he knew so well . . .

Polycarp

A Christian is not lord of his own life, but he has time only for God.

This is the work of God — and it will be yours too, when you fulfil your destiny.

By grace I trust that you are ready to do a good work for God . . .

Farewell in the Lord.
Ignatius

WHEN Polycarp read this letter for the first time, he had prayed: 'Lord Jesus, help me to do a good work for God', and he thought about his friend Ignatius.
That was the last time he had heard from him.

'Po-ly-carp! Po-ly-carp! Po-ly-carp!' . . . the crowd shouted.

Polycarp felt as if he was waking up after a dream.

INTO THE ARENA

WHY was Polycarp standing in the stadium?
What had happened to him?

SOMEBODY had betrayed Polycarp.
Soldiers had come to arrest him for preaching about Jesus.

When the soldiers arrived, Polycarp asked if he could have time to pray. The soldiers listened as he prayed. They had never heard anyone pray the way he did.

Then they took him away in a chariot. They asked him many questions. At first they had been gentle. But then they became impatient. They demanded that he would say Caesar, the Roman Emperor, was Lord.

'Why won't you say "Caesar is Lord", you foolish, stubborn old man?', they asked.

Polycarp said nothing. What was there to say?
How could he say, 'Caesar is Lord'?
Caesar was only the Emperor. Jesus is Lord.

Then the soldiers took hold of Polycarp again and brought him in their chariot to the stadium. Although he was an old man, they threw him out of the chariot onto the ground.

When he stood up he found himself at the entrance to the arena.
There was nowhere to hide.

Slowly Polycarp made his way into the arena.

That was when the crowd saw him, and started chanting his name . . .

'Po-ly-carp . . . Po-ly-carp . . . Po-ly-carp . . .'

Polycarp looked up . . . In the centre of the stadium stood the Proconsul. He was an important official of the mighty Roman Empire. His job was to make sure that everything in Smyrna pleased the Emperor Antony.

The name of the Proconsul was Statius Quadratus.

The Proconsul held up his hand. Everyone became very quiet.

'Are you Polycarp?' asked the Proconsul.
'Yes', said Polycarp, 'I am.'

'Are you a Christian?' asked the Proconsul.
'Yes, I am', replied Polycarp.

'You are an old man, Polycarp.
'You know that you must say "Caesar is Lord." If you will not, you know what will happen', the Proconsul said.
'I know', said Polycarp calmly. 'I have always known.'

The Proconsul raised his voice. He was beginning to get angry. Did this old man not understand?

The Proconsul shouted now.

'Swear by Caesar! Say "Caesar is Lord." Say "Away with those who deny Roman gods" . . . and we will let you go. Deny Jesus and you will be safe.'

THE crowd had been shouting,
 'Away with those who deny the Roman gods!'

But now they were silent.

The people in the front rows leaned forward.

They all wanted to hear Polycarp's answer.

'Are you telling me to say, "Away with those who deny the Roman gods"?' Polycarp asked.

Polycarp knew that the Lord was with him.

He would be strong one more time.

POLYCARP'S hand pointed in the direction of the crowd.

Looking round at them, he spoke to the Proconsul.

There seemed to be a slight smile on his lips.

He spoke up so that everyone could hear . . .

'AWAY with those who deny the true God!' he said.

'Swear that the Emperor Antony is Lord, you fool!'

'Swear! Swear! Swear!' the Proconsul shouted.

THE EMPEROR ANTONY

Faithful to Jesus

As Polycarp stood before the Proconsul, he knew what the Lord Jesus wanted him to say . . .

'I will swear only this:
For 86 years I have served Christ.
He has done me no harm!
How can I deny Jesus who is
my Saviour?'

'**S**WEAR! You fool, Swear!' yelled the Proconsul.

'Don't you know who I am and what I can do to you?'

'**Y**OU don't understand who I am', said Polycarp.

'I am a Christian. If you want to learn what that means, fix the day and I will tell you . . .'

'I have had enough of you, Polycarp', said the Proconsul . . . 'I will bring in wild beasts to devour you . . .'

'Bring them in', said Polycarp defiantly.

Polycarp had recently had a dream about what might happen to him. There were no lions in the dream! He would not be thrown to the lions. Instead he would be burned.

'Since you despise the beasts', said the Proconsul, 'I will bring fire. Perhaps you will fear fire!'

'Bring fire, then', Polycarp said. 'Your fire will last only a short time. It is not the fire to be feared. But there is a fire you should fear . . . the fire of the judgment of God . . . Do what you want to me . . . I will be safe in the hands of heaven.'

THE Proconsul was amazed. But he was also furious. He turned to speak to his herald.

The crowd hushed again.

Then the herald proclaimed in a loud voice.

' Polycarp says, "I am a Christian."'

Again, he said, even more loudly,

' Polycarp says, "I am a Christian."'

Yet again he shouted out,

' Polycarp says, "I am a Christian."'

WHEN the crowd heard these words, they went wild with anger.

They shouted . . .

'This is the leader of the Christians. This is the teacher of the church. He pulls down our gods. He teaches us not to sacrifice to them. Pull Polycarp down. Make him a sacrifice! Bring on the lions! The lions! Polycarp to the lions!'

BUT Roman law said that such a thing could not happen when the Great Games were over.

When the crowd learned this they shouted out,

'Burn him then! Burn him! Burn Polycarp!'

A fire was prepared in a hurry.

Polycarp calmly walked into the middle of the great pile of wood.

Some people wanted to nail him to a wooden stake because they wanted to make sure he would not run away and escape.

'Leave me as I am', Polycarp said.

'I will not try to escape. My Lord is able to keep me by his power in this fire. He is stronger than any of your nails.'

So they tied Polycarp with ropes.

POLYCARP lifted his eyes up to heaven.

As the men lit the fire he began to pray:

'O Lord God Almighty,
You are the Father of your Son Jesus Christ.
Through him we have come to know you.
You are God of the angels and of all powers.
You are Lord of all you have made.
You are Lord of all those who live in your presence.

Lord, I thank you.
You have counted me worthy of this day and hour.

You have made me one of your martyrs.
You have allowed me to drink of Christ's sufferings.
You will allow me to share in the triumph of his resurrection.

Lord, may I be received today into your presence.
You have promised this.
You never lie.

Lord I praise you and worship you.
I pray through Jesus Christ your Son.
He lives with you.
You live with him and with the Holy Spirit.

You are the living God today and forever more.

Amen.'

POLYCARP was burned to death.

He had served the Lord Jesus for 86 years.

It was about 2 o'clock in the afternoon.

It was probably on the 22nd of February in the year 156 A.D.

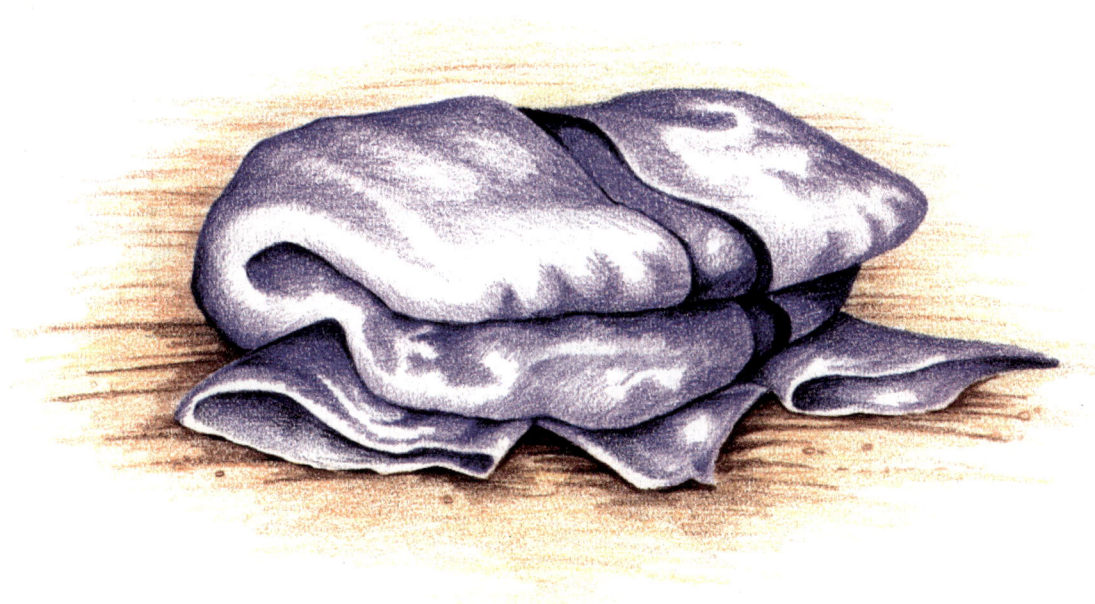

SOME of Polycarp's friends were there in the stadium. They saw everything and wrote down what had happened to their leader.

Later they wrote . . .

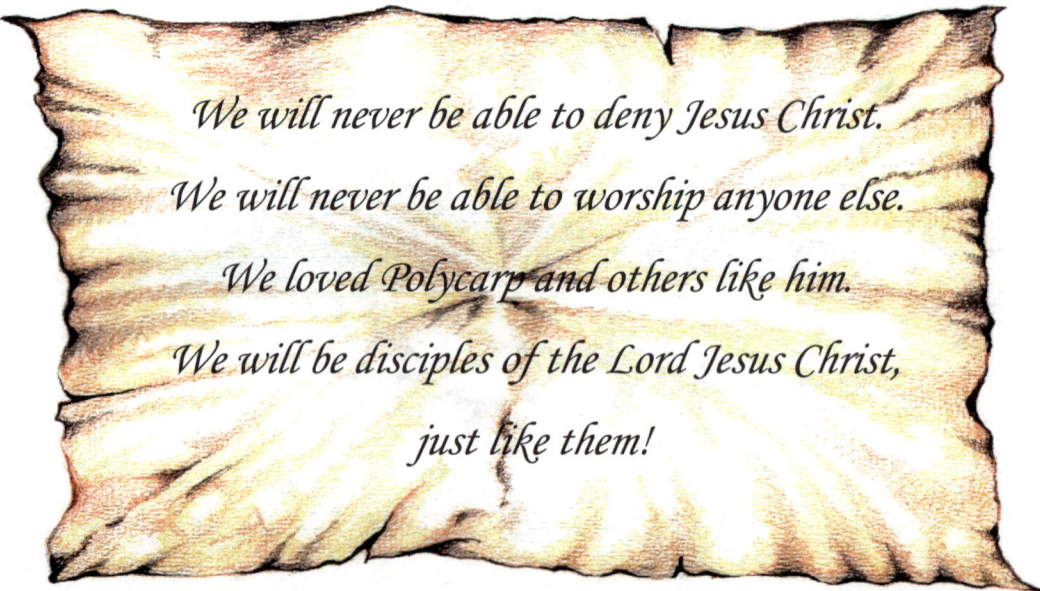

We will never be able to deny Jesus Christ.
We will never be able to worship anyone else.
We loved Polycarp and others like him.
We will be disciples of the Lord Jesus Christ,
just like them!

LEARNING FROM POLYCARP

JESUS said,

'Whoever does not bear his cross and come after me cannot be my disciple.'*

That does not mean that every disciple will be called to die for Jesus. But it did mean that for Polycarp. The Lord Jesus gave him special strength. We know that he can make us strong too if people turn against us because we love Jesus.

THE name Polycarp comes from two Greek words: *polus* (which means 'much') and *karpos* (which means 'fruit'). *Polus-karpos* (Poly-carp) means 'Much Fruit'.

Perhaps his father and mother gave him that name because they had learned that Jesus said to his disciples:

'I am the vine; you are the branches.
Whoever abides in me and I in him, he it is that bears *much fruit*,
for apart from me you can do nothing.'†

Jesus promises us that when we trust him and stay close to him he will help us to serve him. We will have 'much fruit' too — just like Polycarp.

---

* Luke chapter 14 verse 27.

† John chapter 15 verse 5.

POLYCARP was a Christian who had 'much fruit'.

His Christian friends became stronger because of him.

They loved Jesus more because of him.

And they learned this from Polycarp . . .

    Jesus is worth living for and he is worth dying for!

ABOUT POLYCARP OF SMYRNA

Polycarp of Smryna – The Man whose Faith Lasted is a true story.

Polycarp lived in Smyrna from about 70 A.D. to about 156 A.D.

Smyrna was an important city in the Roman Province of Asia Minor and had a population of about 90,000 people. It is now called Izmir and is in the country of Turkey.

Polycarp grew up in a Christian home.

He really did say those wonderful words on the day he was killed. He had trusted, loved, and served the Lord Jesus Christ since he was a boy.

Polycarp did actually meet the Apostle John and was taught by him.

He knew Ignatius of Antioch. You can read about him in *Ignatius of Antioch – The Man who Faced Lions*. Ignatius visited Polycarp when he was on a journey to Rome. He later sent the letter that Polycarp kept.

Polycarp was also the teacher of Irenaeus. You can read about him in *Irenaeus of Lyons – The Man who Wrote Books*.

We know about what happened to Polycarp because the Christians in Smyrna wrote to their friends to tell them what had happened to the minister they loved so much.

HEROES OF THE FAITH

HEROES OF THE FIRST CENTURIES	HEROES OF THE TRUTH	HEROES OF THE DARKNESS AND THE DAWN	HEROES OF THE REFORMATION
IGNATIUS ?-117			
POLYCARP 70-156			
IRENAEUS 130/40-200			
	ATHANASIUS 296-373		
	BASIL OF CAESAREA 329-379		
	GREGORY OF NYSSA 330-395		
	GREGORY OF NAZIANZUS 330-389		
	AUGUSTINE 354-430		
		GOTTSCHALK 805-869	
		ANSELM 1033-1109	
		JOHN WYCLIFFE 1329-84	
		JAN HUSS 1373-1415	
			MARTIN LUTHER 1483-1546
			WILLIAM TYNDALE 1494-1536
			JOHN CALVIN 1509-64
			JOHN KNOX 1514-72

BIRTH OF JESUS
B.C./A.D.
1/1--100--200----300----400----------1100------------1400------------1500--------

TIMELINE

HEROES OF THE PURIFYING	HEROES OF EVANGELISM	HEROES OF THE WORLD	HEROES OF THE 20TH CENTURY

WILLIAM PERKINS 1558-1602
JOHN OWEN 1616-83
JOHN BUNYAN 1628-88

JOHN WESLEY 1703-92
JONATHAN EDWARDS 1703-1758
GEORGE WHITEFIELD 1714-1770

WILLIAM WILBERFORCE 1759-1833
WILLIAM CAREY 1761-1834
HENRY MARTYN 1781-1812
JOHN G. PATON 1824-1907

C. H. SPURGEON 1834-92
D. M. LLOYD-JONES 1899-1981

----1600----------1700----------------------1800----------1900------------2000

A Personal Word to Parents About Heroes of the Faith

Many of our children enjoy having heroes, but they are living in a world that encourages them instead to have 'idols'.

Sometimes, perhaps, the difference is simply a choice of words. But today it is usually more. For the 'idols' our children are encouraged to have — whether by media coverage or peer pressure — are to be 'adored' not because of their character, but because of their image.

By contrast a 'hero' is someone who is much more than a 'personality' about whom we may know little or nothing. A hero is someone who has shown moral fibre, who has overcome difficulties and opposition, who has been tested and has stood firm.

This series is about such people — heroes of the Christian faith — whose lives remind us of the words of Hebrews 13:7: 'Consider the outcome of their way of life, and imitate their faith.'

There are different kinds of heroes. The books in this series reflect the fact that some become heroes by being willing to die for Christ; others because of how they served the church of Christ; yet others because of what they taught about Christ; and others because of where they were prepared to go for Christ.

The **HEROES OF THE FAITH** books are intended to build up into a kind of church family album — pictures of those who, throughout the centuries, have been members of the family of God.

Many of us who are parents wish we could teach our children more about the story of the church, to help them see the privilege of belonging to a spiritual family that stretches back over the centuries and extends to the ends of the earth. This series aims to cover the centuries-long story of the church and to introduce children to heroes of the faith in every period of history.

None of these heroes was perfect — they all recognised their need of the Lord Jesus Christ as their Saviour and Lord. None of them claimed perfect understanding or perfect obedience. But each of them aimed to love the Lord with heart and mind and soul and strength. In that sense they were true heroes.

Many of these heroes were ministers and preachers of the gospel of Jesus Christ. But they were not heroes simply because they were ministers. The word 'minister' means 'servant'. They were people who became leaders in the church; they became heroes because they were servants both of the Lord Jesus and of his people.

I count it a privilege to have the opportunity of introducing your family, and especially your children, to these HEROES OF THE FAITH. May they become heroes too!

SINCLAIR B. FERGUSON